IMAGES
of America

ALONG THE
ST. JOHNS AND
OCKLAWAHA RIVERS

In 1880, General Ulysses S. Grant visited Florida and traveled on the Ocklawaha River in this vessel, the *Osceola*. This engraving was published in February issues of weekly newspapers. Grant was thinking of running for a third term, and one purpose of his visit was to find out how the South viewed him.

IMAGES
of America

ALONG THE ST. JOHNS AND OCKLAWAHA RIVERS

Edward A. Mueller

ARCADIA
PUBLISHING

Published by Arcadia Publishing
Charleston, South Carolina

Library of Congress Catalog Card Number: 99-63434

For all general information contact Arcadia Publishing at:
Telephone 843-853-2070
Fax 843-853-0044
E-Mail sales@arcadiapublishing.com
For customer service and orders:
Toll-Free 1-888-313-2665

Visit us on the Internet at www.arcadiapublishing.com

CONTENTS

ACKNOWLEDGMENTS

Perhaps the most thanks for the photographs in a book like this go to the stereo photographers, known and unknown, who journeyed to Florida well over a century ago and paused to record what they saw on the rivers. To be sure, it was all in earning a living, but their efforts lasted and many of the images presented are certainly due to them. In our time, these images have been preserved in many collections, the most notable of which is that of the Florida Photo Archives in Tallahassee. Joan Morris and Jody Norman maintain and enlarge this collection and the author is sincerely grateful to them.

Members of the Steamship Historical Society of America such as the late C. Bradford Mitchell, the late R. Loren Graham, and the late James and Alice Wilson provided photos, research, and counsel in bygone days. Other friends such as the late Henry Boggs, the late John Lochhead, the late Captain Henry D. DeGrove II and his son H. D. "Bud" DeGrove III were also helpful. Image collectors of old time Florida such as William Dreggors, Robert Cauthen, and Doug Hendricksen deserve credit for their assistance with photographs.

INTRODUCTION

In the early days of the 19th century, transportation by water was significant in how both persons and goods reached Florida. Florida is a peninsula for the most part and is accessible by water on the east, west, and south. There are also many waterways that serve portions of the interior, and this book serves to present some of the pictorial aspects of the vessels, primarily steamboats, and people that used the St. Johns and Ocklawaha Rivers. These two rivers helped convey winter visitors from the north to most areas of northeast Florida, and in their time were most significant in doing so. Certainly in bygone days, both the St. Johns and Ocklawaha Rivers were important factors in the development of Florida as they provided the natural waterways upon which tourists and settlers could travel, "see the sights," remember what they had seen, and either tell their neighbors or return themselves to settle down.

Robert Fulton is generally regarded as achieving the first commercially successful steamboat operation in 1807 on the Hudson River. Since that time, steamboat development had progressed significantly into all parts of the young United States, including the South. The cities of Charleston, South Carolina and Savannah, Georgia were key transportation centers, and many sailing ships and steamboats destined for Florida departed from these two cities.

THE ST. JOHNS RIVER. In the mid-1830s, when this story begins, the principal Northeast Florida settlements were at Fernandina, Jacksonville, Palatka, and St. Augustine. These areas were small, but all were port cities and were served by water craft. In 1830, Florida's population was 34,730 and Duval County (Jacksonville) had 1,970 persons. It is obvious that there was not much of a local population base to support water transportation by steamboats. However, as time went on and the area grew, frequent steamboat connections between the St. Johns River area and Savannah came into being. The first steamboat arrived in Jacksonville in May 1829, and was *George Washington*, a Charleston-built steamboat only 90 feet long. She was to be the first of many to bring winter visitors to Florida. The next steamboat to visit Jacksonville was *Florida*, a 104-foot sidewheeler built in Savannah in 1834.

Of all the natural waterways in Florida, the St. Johns River was the most promising and best adapted to steamboat use. Unlike most other American rivers, this river flows from south to north. Fed by flowing springs, it provides access to 7,000 square miles of land that had great potential for agriculture and lumbering. The current is relatively moderate with a fall of only 20 feet in 200 miles. The river consists of a series of long lakes, and the area rainfall is such that the river and most of its tributaries, including the Ocklawaha River, have adequate water levels most of the year. The most grievous obstacle to navigation was a system of shifting sand bars at the mouth of the river where the St. Johns joined the Atlantic. This severely limited navigation to vessels having drafts of eight feet or less. Many other areas of the river, however, had depths of water sufficient to dock those vessels that could get across the bars at the river's mouth.

In the mid-1830s, railroads were not yet a factor in transportation since low cost steel for rails and engines was not available. Not until the 1850s would a railroad even be built in East Florida. Roads were almost non-existent. In 1821, when Florida was created as a territory, the two principal roads were the British "Kings Road" which ran from the St. Marys River to New Smyrna via Jacksonville and St. Augustine. The other road went from St. Augustine to Pensacola and had been built by the Spanish. Therefore, the natural waterways had to suffice to transport persons and goods to and around Florida.

THE OCKLAWAHA RIVER. Like the St. Johns River, the Ocklawaha River flows north and enters the St. Johns opposite Welaka. The river's headwaters are in the lakes in central Florida, and Leesburg on Lake Harris is generally regarded as the head of navigation. The chief destination for the unique recessed-sternwheel propulsion vessels on the Ocklawaha, however, was Silver Springs, then as now a tourist destination.

The Ocklawaha River's controlling depth is only a few feet, and it is especially narrow from the junction with Silver Springs Run to the lakes area further south. The bordering areas are mostly swamp-like, heavily forested and unsettled. Even today, the river is of a primitive nature, and, once into it, the traveler is in another land and another time.

In steamboat times, the first small vessels to use the river were built in Jacksonville during the 1850s. Little is known of their careers, and it would not be until after the War Between the States that navigation on the Ocklawaha would emerge as a transportation factor of some importance.

A Vermonter, Hubbard L. Hart, originally came to Florida for health reasons but started his transportation career by running a stage line to Tampa. Just before the war, Hart bought into several steamboats and worked for the Confederacy, in blockade running and moving goods on the St. Johns and Ocklawaha Rivers. During the conflict, the Ocklawaha River became clogged with various objects such as fallen trees, overhanging vegetation, and the like. After the conflict, Hart achieved contracts with the State of Florida to clear away these obstructions, receiving grants of land for doing these tasks.

There was some competition among steamboat owners for trade on the river. Confederate Captain Henry Gray emerged as a player, and a Jacksonville-area doctor S.J. Bouknight also ran some vessels. However, Hart dominated until his death in 1895.

Trips on the river usually started at Palatka on the St. Johns from where it was a 25-mile jaunt to the mouth of the Ocklawaha and then an 85- to 100-mile trip to the head of navigation near Leesburg. A nine-mile detour on Silver Springs Run brought one to Silver Springs, and most winter visitors chose to stop there. There was much less continuing traffic further south, and, in subsequent years, the advent of railroads to that area obviated the need for steamboats to bring freight and passengers there.

The following pages present pictorial evidence of the river vessels and their obvious influence on the area. The captions serve to present details of these steamboats and sailing ships that were once so significant but are now largely forgotten.

One

THE ST. JOHNS RIVER: THE EARLY DAYS

Andrew Jackson, the first American governor of the Territory of Florida and later President of the United States, was the man for whom the city of Jacksonville was named.

Darlington was an early 1849 Charleston-built steamboat owned by Captain Jacob Brock and was one of the first vessels on the St. Johns River, plying between Jacksonville and Sanford. This is a John Fryant sketch made from an old photograph, showing her at Welaka.

The Savannah-built *Welaka* made weekly trips between Savannah and Jacksonville. She is seen here under the operation of Captain Nick King, entering the St. Johns River. She was lost at the river's junction with the Atlantic Ocean in 1857. Fortunately, there was no loss of life.

The racing yacht *America*, commemorated here in topical sheet music, was captured in the St. Johns by Union forces during the Civil War. She was to be a blockade runner for the Confederacy, and had been "bottled up" in the river.

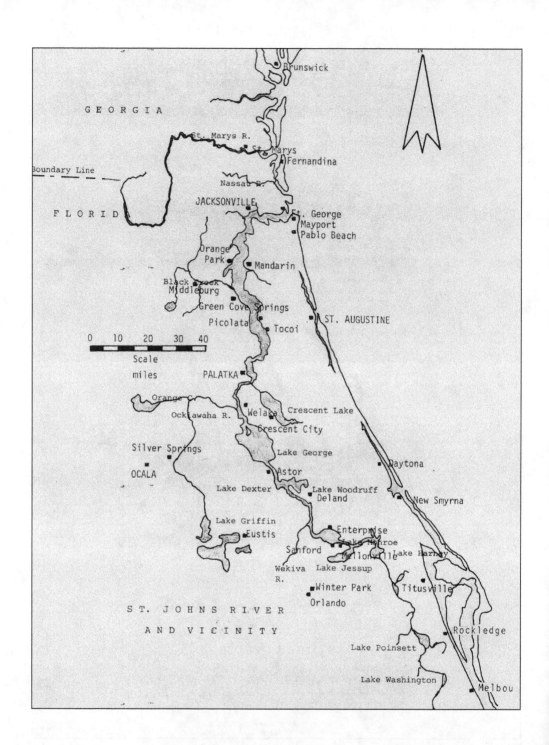

One of the early lighthouses constructed at the mouth of the St. Johns River was a victim of erosion. Later lighthouses were placed farther inland, and one survives to this day.

Jacksonville is pictured here shortly after the Civil War. This building is on the north side of Bay Street and is "guarded" by a Union sentry.

Sylph was a former Brooklyn ferry that came to Florida and was in local service near Jacksonville in the late 1860s. A very unusual-looking vessel, her furnaces and stack are placed at the rear of her paddlewheels rather than before the wheels, the usual placement.

A Palatka taxidermist and curio store where winter visitors arriving by steamboat had the opportunity to purchase souvenirs. Notice the little boy in front, sitting on the stuffed alligator with its jaws propped open.

Starlight was a wooden steamboat plying between Jacksonville and Sanford. She burned in 1878 on Lake Monroe at Sanford with no loss of life. Note her paddlewheel box details.

The pride of the DeBary Line was their iron-hulled *Frederick DeBary* of the early 1880s. After a year of operation, she burned at her downtown Jacksonville wharf. This painting by Bill Trotter shows her as having been rebuilt. She was lengthened and re-engined in the process.

Steamboats were often depicted on postcards. This is such a postcard image of the *Frederick DeBary*. Note the eagle on top of the pilot house, a frequent feature of St. Johns steamboats.

Two

AFTER THE WAR
BETWEEN THE STATES

The wooden, Jacksonville-built *Hattie* (*c.* 1861) is seen here at Brock's shipyard. She was named after Captain Jacob Brock's daughter and carried the U.S. mail.

Dictator was a sturdy, wooden sidewheeler that made weekly trips between Charleston, Savannah, Jacksonville, and Palatka from 1866 until the end of the 1870s. She saw service for Union forces during the war.

An 1875 stereo view depicts the Savannah-built *Lizzie Baker* at Green Cove Springs. She was one of the few twin-stacked sidewheelers on the river and made a weekly round trip between Savannah and Palatka.

Rosa, an iron-hulled sidewheeled steamboat built in Wilmington, Delaware, was owned by the DeBary-Baya Merchants line. She was on the St. Johns during the 1880s.

Count Frederick DeBary bought the wooden *Florence* from Captain Charles Brock and renamed her *Anita* after his granddaughter. She ran for many years on the DeBary-Baya Merchants Line. Note the beam structure over the paddlewheel area. This supported the single-cylinder engine that operated both wheels.

Shipping yellow pine and cypress lumber and timber was the principal export business in East Florida for several decades. These two stereo views taken from the National Hotel show the Jacksonville waterfront, where much of this activity occurred.

The Mathews Block on downtown Bay Street in the 1870s is pictured above, in a stereo view by the Anthony Company. Below, old time Bay Street in downtown Jacksonville as seen in the late 1860s or early 1870s. All the streets were unpaved and, for the most part, everyone walked to their destinations.

FOR FLORIDA, THE

First-Class New-York Built Steamers

DICTATOR, - **Capt. Vogel,**
CITY POINT, - **Capt. Fitzgerald,**

Connect at CHARLESTON and SAVANNAH with the New York Steamers and Northern Trains for

SAVANNAH,	*HIBERNIA,*
FERNANDINA,	*MAGNOLIA,*
JACKSONVILLE,	*GREEN COVE Springs,*
St. AUGUSTINE,	*PALATKA,*

INCLUDING ALL LANDINGS ON THE ST. JOHN'S RIVER.

CONNECT AT PALATKA WITH STEAMERS FOR ENTERPRISE, MELLONVILLE, SANFORD, AND INDIAN RIVER, ALSO WITH STEAMERS FOR THE OCKLAWAHA RIVER.

A sufficient number of the CHOICEST STATE-ROOMS are reserved for Passengers by the NEW YORK STEAMERS.

Passengers will find on these Steamers every comfort and convenience— a first-class table, and polite and attentive employees.

For Freight or passage, apply in New York to Agents of Charleston and Savannah Steamship Lines.

This advertising card for Florida-bound vessel dates to 1874. Captain Leo Vogel and Captain James W. Fitzgerald had significant river careers.

The Brock House was located at Enterprise, on Lake Monroe on the St. Johns River. The passenger and freight wharf leading to the well-known hostelry has tracks for wheeled carts for the interchange of traffic.

Although of poor quality, this *c.* 1876 photograph shows the *General Sedgwick* at the Tocoi wharf, where passengers could transfer directly to the St. Johns Railway for an arduous three-hour journey to St. Augustine.

Two children view Jacob Brock's *Florence*, shown here at a landing on the St. Johns. A wooden sidewheeler, she was powered with a single, one-cylinder walking-beam engine. Later renamed *Anita*, she was used by the DeBary Merchants Line.

Three

HEAVY RIVER TRAFFIC
IN THE 1870S AND 1880S

Former President General U.S. Grant visited Florida in 1880 and used this sidewheeler to get to the St. Johns and, later, the *Osceola* on the Ocklawaha River. This engraving is from a February 1880 *Harper's Weekly*.

The Florida East Coast Railway built the first bridge across the river at Jacksonville in 1888. It was a swing bridge that opened for water traffic such as this three-masted lumber schooner being towed easterly by a local tug.

When a steamboat was not available, visitors could take this bus to go from Green Cove Springs to Jacksonville or vice versa. The trip by water was considered more comfortable, however.

The Pittsburgh-built *Chattahoochee* carried heavy loads on the St. Johns River. She was a steel-hulled sternwheeler with wooden upper works where passengers were housed. Cargo and machinery were placed on the lower deck. Wood was used as fuel.

Chattahoochee, with a varied freight load, is pictured here at a wharf near Georgetown. Note the pier built out into the river. The river was shallow near the shore, and piers were needed to serve steamboats. The shed was used to keep passengers or goods out of the rain.

The steel-hulled *Chattahoochee* of the early 1880s served initially on the Apalachicola and Chattahoochee Rivers before coming to the St. Johns in 1883 to run with Henry B. Plant's People's Line. This sketch is by Samuel Ward Stanton, who was lost at sea on the *Titanic*.

This 1880s view along the St. Johns (looking westerly) at Jacksonville shows lumber schooners and the *Tuskawilla* in the foreground.

The beautiful steam launch *Princess*, shown here on Rice Creek near Palatka, was often in use for local daylight excursions. She has stopped here to be photographed.

Belle of the Coast was a large cotton-carrying Mississippi River steamboat that came to the St. Johns in 1885 to compete with the predominate Eastern-style steamboats. She was unsuccessful and went back to New Orleans and the cotton trade after a few months.

During the peak of the steamboat days in 1884 and 1885, Captain Ed Maddy brought his sternwheeled *Chesapeake* from the Ohio River to the St. Johns to share in the short-lived steamboat bonanza. She was probably the first vessel to have electric lights on the St. Johns.

The two-masted *Meta* was a local pilot boat that met incoming vessels at the mouth of the St. Johns. River pilots would board these ships and pilot them to downtown Jacksonville. *Meta* was purchased from New Jersey interests and served later in the Tampa area.

Six St. Johns River "bar" pilots as seen here on their pilot schooner *Meta*. From left to right are Sam Singleton Jr., Charlie Daniels, an unidentified woman, Joseph Mickler, Arthur Spalding Sr., Arthur Spalding Jr., and Sam Singleton Sr.

Volunteer, a Jacksonville towing vessel, displays the Confederate flag and one with her house insignia, probably during a river procession after the turn of the century.

The small, wooden launch *Hyacinth* is pictured at the "ghost" town of St. Francis, Florida.

The wooden Duval Hotel, gingerbread and all, served winter visitors in the 1880s and thereafter, until the structure was lost in a 1901 fire. Note the horse-drawn vehicles. This is a postcard view from the 1880s.

This old stereo photo depicts the S.B. Hubbard hardware and crockery store on Bay Street in Jacksonville in the 1880s. One could buy almost anything at Hubbards.

33

City of Jacksonville, underway on the St. Johns, was considered the best all-around steamboat on the river. Her usual running mate was the *Frederick DeBary*.

City of Jacksonville was an iron-hulled Wilmington, Delaware-built steamboat that served for almost 40 years on the St. Johns. She often went to the Boston area in summers to serve the heavy excursion trade to the beaches there.

An "action" shot of *City of Jacksonville* shows her lower deck and the passenger quarters on the upper deck. Note the wire safety netting below the railing, which was designed to prevent children from falling overboard.

City of Jacksonville is underway with all her decorative flags flying as she makes one of her tri-weekly, overnight trips between Jacksonville and Sanford.

TIME CARD
— OF —
Steamer JOHN SYLVESTER
AND CONNECTIONS.

Read Down.	SEASON 1888.	Read Up.
8.30 a.m.	Lv. Jacksonville ....Ar	7.00 p.m.
10.30 "	Ar. Green Cove Spring ...Lv	5.15 "
11.45 "	" { Tocoi, {	4.15 "
12.30 noon	" { St. Augustine, {	2.30 "
1.15 p.m.	" Palatka , ... "	2.15 "
1.30 "	" Rolleston .... "	1.45 "
	St. Johns & Halifax R. R.	
5.15 "	" Ormond .... "	7.45 a.m.
5.30 "	" Daytona Lv	7.30 "
Lv. Palatka. Florida Southern Railway..		2.00 p.m.
Ar. Gainesville, " " ..		5.00 "
" Ocala, " " ..		5.30 "
" Leesburg, " " ..		6.30 "
Lv. Palatka (Rail)................		2.15 p.m.
Ar. Enterprise (Rail)		4.25 "
" Sanford "		4.50 "
Lv. St. Augustine for Palatka (via Tocoi), 10.30 a.m.		
" Palatka for St. Augustine		2.15 p.m.

Breakfast, Jacksonville. Dinner, St. Augustine and Palatka. Supper, Sanford, Enterprise and other points beyond Palatka.

ST. JOHNS RIVER,
SPECIAL DAYLIGHT SERVICE.

The Elegant Fast, New York Steamer,

JOHN SYLVESTER

Leaves JACKSONVILLE 8.30 A.M.
FROM ASTOR WHARF,
MAKING ROUND TRIP DAILY, EXCEPT SUNDAY.

RIVER and RAIL CONNECTIONS
— TO ALL —
SOUTH FLORIDA POINTS.
THE TOURISTS' ROUTE.

For Information, Passage Tickets, &c., apply to
E. W. EBBETS, Pass. Agent,
74 West Bay Street,
At Office on Wharf, or Purser on board Steamer.
C. V. H. POST. Gen'l Agent.

POST'S DAY LINE

Distances on St. Johns River
FROM JACKSONVILLE

TO	MILES.
Orange Park............	13
Mandarin....................	15
Hibernia...................	23
Magnolia.................	28
Green Cove Spring	30
Picolata.................	46
Tocoi—for St. Augustine........	49
Federal Point	60
Palatka...................	75
Rolleston................	77
San Mateo	78
Welaka	93
Lake George.............	105
Astor................	120
DeLand..........	145
Blue Springs	155
Sanford................	175
Enterprise	180

STEAMER CONNECTIONS AT PALATKA.

Steamers for Ocklawaha River, leaving Palatka at **2** P. M.

Steamer GEORGIA, for San Mateo, Welaka, Georgetown and Drayton Island.

And Steamer CURLEW, for Orange Mills, and Crescent City Steamer, all leaving Palatka at **2** P. M.

Upper St. Johns River Steamers for Enterprise and Sanford, leaving Palatka at **9** P. M.

These excerpts are advertisements for the Post Line's *John Sylvester*. The *Eliza Hancox* was her running mate.

John Sylvester was a fast river steamboat and ran for the Post Day Line. During summer she was employed on New York waters, and in winter, she was on the St. Johns.

The Post Line's *Eliza Hancox*, running mate of the *John Sylvester*, is seen here leaving the Magnolia Hotel at Magnolia on the St. Johns River. Note the walking-beam engine as well as the ornamental gazebo on the hotel pier.

Hanaro T. Baya purchased this ex-lighthouse tender, *Tulip*, in the 1870s, renamed her *Magnolia*, and used her on daylight commuter runs to Green Cove Springs and to Pilot Town and Mayport. Originally named the *I.N. Seymour*, she saw service for the Union during the Civil War.

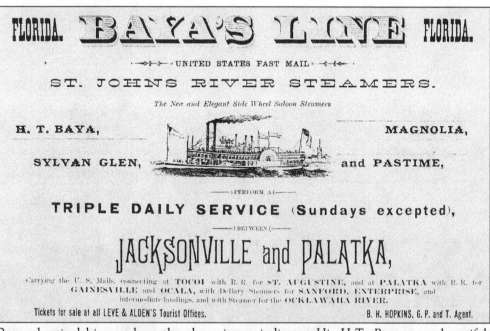

Baya advertised his vessels as the above image indicates. His *H.T. Baya* was a beautiful, Philadelphia-built craft, but she only served a few months on the St. Johns. *Sylvan Glen* was a former New York-area commuter vessel.

Four

Ferries, Excursion, and Towing Vessels

The decorative, wooden tug *Biscayne* was owned by Captains Henry and Charles Fozzard.

A view from the Brock House lawn at Enterprise on Lake Monroe shows the iron-hulled *Frederick DeBary* departing from the Brock House wharf. The Brock House was the principal feature of Enterprise.

The diminutive launch *Undine* is seen here on a hunting expedition at Blue Springs in Volusia County, Florida. Blue Springs is a Florida state park today on the St. Johns River at Orange City.

The iron-hulled *St. Johns* was the largest and best steamboat that ever came to the St. Johns River. Based in Charleston, she made two round trips per week in the winter season between Charleston and Palatka from 1878 to 1882.

In this picture of the railroad/steamboat wharf at Sanford in the 1880s, the *Waunita* (pictured) was to ply the upper river. The *Okeehumkee* (behind *Waunita*) was usually seen on the Ocklawaha River. The rails on the wharf often carried passenger railroad cars to meet the St. Johns River steamboats.

This 1893 print of the *City of Jacksonville* on the St. Johns is romantically entitled "Moonlight on the St. Johns." Note the star on the stack.

Aquatic hyacinths were a problem to navigation, and *City of Jacksonville* struggles with them at a way landing on the river. Hyacinths often impeded steamboat travel and were a great nuisance.

Railroad and steamboat entrepreneur Henry B. Plant named this vessel *Margaret* after his second wife. The steamboat was originally the *George R. Kelsey*, and she ran on the St. Johns River in the early 1880s under both names.

This is a rendering of *Louise*, a sidewheel transfer steamboat of the St. Augustine and Palatka Railroad (at Palatka). Until a bridge was provided, vessels such as this had to suffice.

Mystic was a wooden sidewheel commuter and excursion vessel that went between Mayport and Pilot Town at the mouth of the river to downtown Jacksonville. She was powered by a walking-beam engine.

The sidewheel tug *Flora Temple* was powered by a walking-beam engine and often towed rafts of logs on the St. Johns River. Her crew was housed in quarters between the sidewheels.

This is a 1920s view, looking southeast, that shows the high-level Acosta bridge (built 1921) in the background and the jackknife FEC Railway drawbridge in the foreground. The Sanford-bound *City of Jacksonville* is passing through both bridges.

In the 1900s, before bridges were built across the St. Johns River, double-ended ferries served to carry passengers and vehicles across the river between downtown (north side) and South Jacksonville on the south side. This shows the wooden, Jacksonville-built *Duval*.

Exporting yellow pine lumber was big business at Palatka and Jacksonville, and three-, four-, and five-masted schooners were the typical cargo ships used for this purpose. Shown here is the *Lottie Russell* in a 1900 photo.

A two-masted Spanish sailing ship is seen at Pilot Town on the St. Johns, *c.* 1900. She carries "square" sails on her foremast and fore-and-aft on the other mast.

The fast, double-ended sailing sloop, *Mack*, was built at Mayport in 1900 for personal recreational purposes.

The steam launch *Agnes K.* arrives at New Berlin in 1900 with a sizeable passenger load. She was primarily used for local service.

The steel-hulled *Crescent*, built at Merrill-Stevens in the early 1900s, ran between Jacksonville or Palatka and Crescent City for many years. She later was found in service on Tampa Bay.

Although quite average-looking in these photos, *Three Friends* was the most famous of the Jacksonville towing vessels. She saw duty as a filibustering vessel in Cuba, a dispatch boat in the Spanish-American War, and a salvage tug before her last career as a conventional harbor tug.

The launch-type, Jacksonville-built *Clara* approaches her destination of Sanford in the early 1900s. The shed on the wharf is to keep passengers and freight out of the weather as needed.

This is a side view of the *Three Friends* with a crowd aboard her. She was often used as the "ceremonial" vessel on the river, and had been owned by a former Florida governor, Napoleon Bonaparte Broward.

Two views (1916–1917) show the wooden *Magnolia* being constructed at the Anderson shipyard located on the south side of the river. The Independent Day Line commissioned her for their local commuter and excursion service.

Captain Charles Edward Garner, owner of the Independent Day Line, ran a successful commuter service from Green Cove Springs and also employed his *May Garner* and *Magnolia* on local excursions.

The pilot house of the *May Garner*, Captain Henry D. DeGrove Sr., and his young son Henry II are all seen here. Both men were involved in steamboating all of their lives.

The St. Johns River Independent Day Line's *Magnolia* carried a goodly number of excursionists in the 1920s. Note the "D" in her house flag, signifying "Day Line."

Here can be seen the pilothouse and entryway of the *Magnolia* as she waits for excursionists to board in downtown Jacksonville in the 1920s.

May Garner spends some time at a local Jacksonville shipyard for maintenance work. Small vessels were pulled out of the water and placed on a marine railway, as shown here.

The propeller steamboat *May Garner* was named for owner C.E. Garner's daughter, May. The steamboat was a fixture on the St. Johns for many years.

Captain and Mrs. Henry D. DeGrove leave *Magnolia* along with other passengers after an excursion. Note the stacked cords of wood fuel at left.

Mrs. Henry (Carla) DeGrove II and Captain Mike Coleman are pictured aboard the *City of Jacksonville*, c. 1920.

This odd-looking vehicle served to advertise the Independent Day Line of the DeGroves and Garner and is shown here on Bay Street in downtown Jacksonville. It was used to attract tourists and arouse attention.

The Stowe family is pictured at their Mandarin home. From left to right are the three Stowe daughters, the well-known author of *Uncle Tom's Cabin,* Harriet Beecher Stowe, and Professor (Reverend) Calvin Stowe. Harriet Beecher Stowe often met the excursion boats and gave oranges to the passengers.

Pope Catlin was a Brunswick, Georgia-based wooden sidewheeled steamboat that came to Jacksonville and ran as a ferry during a time when ferries were in short supply.

One of the latter-day ferries going from downtown Jacksonville to South Jacksonville, these ferries carried both passengers and cars. A bridge built in 1940 put those vessels out of business.

Ravenswood was a double-ended sidewheel ferry that used to carry passengers and vehicles between downtown Jacksonville and South Jacksonville at the turn of the century.

A freighter at Palatka on the St. Johns is seen with a barge alongside. The upper works of *Lavinia*, a local excursion vessel, are in the foreground.

In the 1950s, ferries were provided at Mayport near the mouth of the St. Johns. Shown here are two, *Buccaneer* and *Sirius*, that were operated by the old Florida State Road Department. The tourist "Buccaneer" Trail was on both sides of the river and ferries provided the missing link.

Jean Lafitte, a wooden double-ended ferry, operated at Mayport for many years. The *Buccaneer* eventually replaced the *Jean Lafitte*.

Entrance to Clyde Line Dock, Jacksonville, Fla.

Another view of the Clyde Line docks in Jacksonville show the easy access to railroads, wagons, and horse-drawn vehicles. Note the two ships awaiting cargo. Several sailings were made each week, and it was a delightful sea trip to and from the south to northern destinations.

Entrance to Clyde Line Docks, Jacksonville, Fla.

The Clyde Line coastal liners plied between New York, Charleston, and Jacksonville. Shown here are their docks in Jacksonville. Easy transfer of cargo to and from railroad cars occurred because of the proximity of one to the other.

62

This view looking south shows the covered sheds for steamboat cargoes, a ferry (middle right) that is about to leave, and a small excursion vessel (center) approaching her downtown wharf. The FEC Railway bridge is in the background.

The Clyde Line docks in Jacksonville featured easy access to both railroads and horse-drawn vehicles. There was room for the storage of cargo that was awaiting loading aboard the coastal liners, and railroad cars could be run directly onto the docks next to the vessels.

During World War I, the various ship-building companies in Jacksonville employed this wooden *St. Johns* to carry their workers across the river to their jobs. Note the unusual hog chains and bracing.

The Clyde Line pier at the foot of Hogan Street also provided seating during lunch time for the day laborers employed in the vicinity.

Five

LAST DAYS AND RECENT ACTIVITY

Palatka also used ferries to cross the St. Johns. The very crude *Transport of Palatka* served that purpose in the late 1880s and 1890s before a bridge was built.

Looking south from Bay Street in downtown Jacksonville, the river ferry to South Jacksonville and Dixieland Park is at left, at the end of the street, c. 1910. Trolleys ran on Bay Street; note the tracks.

The first viaduct over railroads in Florida was built in Jacksonville and served to facilitate cargo interchange between railroads and ships by separating the railroads from the vehicular traffic. This postcard view shows the railroad yards (foreground) and the viaduct (background).

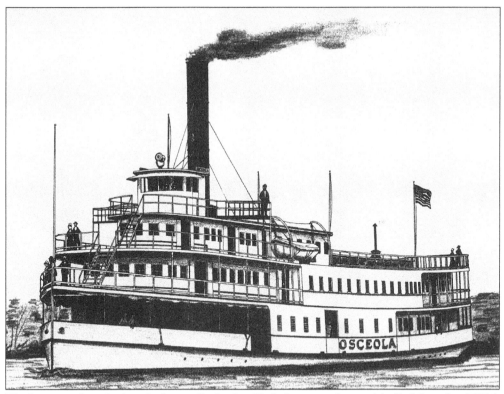

The last steamboat built in Jacksonville for the Clyde Line was the steel-hulled *Osceola* of 1914. She replaced the *Frederick DeBary*, which went to Tampa. This sketch is by Mike Stevens.

Osceola was a recessed sternwheel vessel, probably the largest ever built of this type. Note the distinctive wake shown in this view.

After steamboating had died out on the St. Johns, the St. Johns River Line was formed, using very homely vessels and surplus diesel engines. The usual run was from Jacksonville to Sanford in the 1930s and 1940s.

River vessels of the St. Johns River Line take cargo off a ocean-going ship tied up at downtown Jacksonville. These vessels also carried "containerized" freight, being some of the first to do so.

Jacksonville's Merrill-Stevens salvage equipment is shown raising the iron-hulled *Billow* after she had sunk in the St. Johns River. Merrill-Stevens was a dominant factor in the marine repair business for over 80 years.

Merrill-Stevens built *Attaquin* in 1898 in Jacksonville. She served most of her working life in the Brunswick, Georgia, area as a local commuter and excursion sidewheel steamboat.

World War II saw 82 Liberty ships built in Jacksonville. The first one completed, *Ponce de Leon*, was under construction for 211 days and was launched at night as the photo shows.

After WW II, many vessels stopped at Merrill-Stevens for routine maintenance. Shown here is a Navy hospital ship on the left, a troop ship in the center, and perhaps a tanker on the right. Local tugs stand by to assist with docking large ships.

Looking north at the Merrill-Stevens shipyard, this view shows the small yachts and other vessels that were berthed or maintained there.

The pleasure yacht *Cooter*, owned by Arthur Stevens of the Merrill-Stevens Corporation, was used for recreation by family and friends. The vessel featured a wooden hull, comfortable living quarters, and a viewing area on the top deck that protected one from the weather .

The American-built Atlantic Ocean liner U.S.S. *Constitution* was idled for several years in the backwater 'old river' that lies to the north of Blount Island. She was later renovated and served for many years in the Hawaiian Islands.

After her career in the South and in New York waters, *St. Johns* was renovated as *Tolchester* and was run on the Chesapeake Bay in the 1930s. She burned in 1941 and was then used as a barge for over two decades.

The *Robert Fulton* was a renowned Hudson River flyer. At the end of her career in the 1950s, she was brought to Jacksonville for conversion to living quarters for wood cutters in the Bahamas. She is shown here before the conversion was begun. Her engines and other machinery have been removed.

River Queen was a short-lived excursion vessel operating in Jacksonville on the St. Johns in the 1970s. The FEC Railway bridge and Acosta bridge are in the background.

A modern-day, local excursion and dinner cruise vessel, the *First Lady* (*of Jacksonville*) awaits her passengers in downtown Jacksonville.

After WW II, the sailing yacht *Sea Cloud*, now named *Angelita* and owned by the Dominican Republic, made Jacksonville her usual home port. Shown here with her topmasts lowered (to get under the St. Johns River bridges), she is being eased into a Merrill-Stevens berth.

Three tugs assist the beautiful, four-masted *Angelita* into her berth at Merrill-Stevens.

The *Sea Cloud* is pictured here at anchor in Jacksonville. Merrill-Stevens maintained her for many years as *Angelita* for the Dominican Republic. She was eventually sold and serves today as a luxury cruise ship in the Caribbean and Mediterranean.

Six

THE OCKLAWAHA RIVER:
THE EARLY DAYS

This rare 1883 photo shows the wooden sidewheeler *Roxie* (which burned a few months after this picture was taken) and the Ocklawaha River *Tuskawilla*, probably at Leesburg.

Here is an exaggerated 1871 version of an Ocklawaha steamboat at Silver Springs.

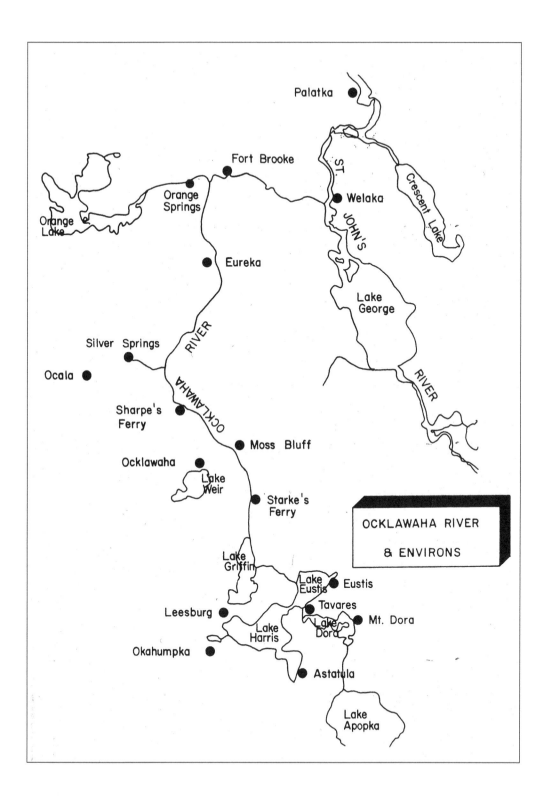

Palatka

Fort Brooke

Orange
Springs

Orange
Lake

Welaka

ST. JOHN'S

Crescent Lake

Eureka

RIVER

Lake
George

Silver Springs

Ocala

OCKLAWAHA

RIVER

Sharpe's
Ferry

Moss Bluff

Ocklawaha

Lake
Weir

Starke's
Ferry

OCKLAWAHA RIVER

& ENVIRONS

Lake
Griffin

Lake
Eustis

Eustis

Tavares

Leesburg

Lake
Dora

Mt. Dora

Okahumpka

Lake
Harris

Astatula

Lake
Apopka

United States Mail.

Change of Proprietorship.

CONCORD

COACHES,

GOOD

HORSES, &C.

PILATKA to TAMPA,

Via Orange Spring, Orange Lake, Ocala, Camp Izard, Augusta, Melendez, Pierceville, and Ft. Taylor.

Stages leave Pilatka and Tampa, Mondays and Thursdays, at 7
A. M., arriving at Tampa and Pilatka, (respectively,) the following Wednesdays and Saturdays; (resting at night, thereby affording Invalids a better opportunity for travelling,) connecting at Tampa with the

N. Orleans and Key West Steamers,
and at Pilatka with the Steam-Boats for Savannah and Charleston.

Also: Intersecting this line, is a Stage from Ocala, via Fleming-ton, Micanopy, and Newnansville, to Alligator.

EXTRA CARRIAGES & HORSES ON HAND,
at Pilatka, to convey Passengers to Micanopy, Flemington, Silver Spring, &c. &c.

ALL EXPRESS BUSINESS PROMPTLY ATTENDED TO.

OFFICE IN PILATKA, AT COL. J. O. DUVAL'S HOTEL.

July, 1855.

H. L. HART, Proprietor.

This 1855 stagecoach poster, from the State Library, recalls a mode of transportation which people nowadays usually associate with this country's West. Pilatka is today's Palatka. Camp Izard was near Dunnellon. Melendez was once the seat of Benton county, today's Hernando county. Alligator is still an important transportation hub, better known as Lake City.

This 1855 broadside advertises Colonel Hubbard L. Hart's stage coach venture, which carried the U.S. Mail and packages between Pilatka (Palatka) and Tampa.

Colonel Hubbard L. Hart devoted most of his adult life to operating a successful line of steamboats on the Ocklawaha River. The "Colonel" title is probably honorary.

As can be seen in this view titled "Look Out Thar," overhanging and bordering tree limbs would often catch river passengers unaware, prompting them to protect themselves.

These two stereo views show the *Griffin*, one of the early Hart vessels, that was named after Lake Griffin located near Leesburg. This vessel was often used for clearing obstacles in the river.

This U.S. mail box along the river
is fastened to a tree; this one is at
Sharpe's Ferry.

Griffin takes on cargo at a way landing on the Ocklawaha River. The large pair of wheels was
used to move heavy logs.

The initial version of the *Ocklawaha* of the mid-1870s was built at Hart's Point in East Palatka, as were most of Hubbard L. Hart's recessed sternwheel steamboats.

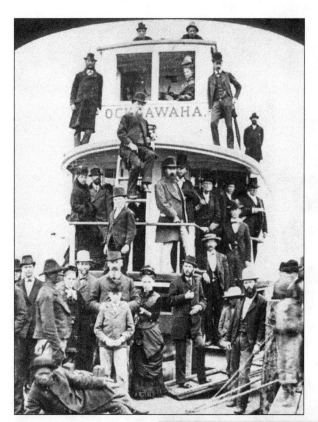

Ocklawaha was eventually rebuilt, and her pilot house was elevated. Captain David Dunham, who constructed most of Hart's steamboats, is next to the letter "O" on the pilot house.

Captain Henry Gray brought out his *Marion* in the mid-1870s, and this illustration from a contemporary article, "The Great South," shows what an artist's imagination can create.

An old stereo view shows Henry Gray's *Marion* at Iola Landing, on the Ocklawaha River .

Travelers on Captain Henry Gray's *Marion* are decked out in their heavy winter clothing and hats, and many are carrying rifles. Even young children took trips on the river; note the nurse and baby in the foreground.

Hubbard L. Hart ran four recessed sternwheel vessels, as this 1890 advertisement indicates. The sketch is typical of these unique steamboats. Cargo and machinery were on the lower deck, passengers on the next deck, and the pilothouse and captain's quarters were atop that deck.

Henry Gray sold his *Marion* to Colonel Hart in 1880, and she was renovated as shown in this side view. Captain Gray is at the door of the pilot house. Gray continued to work for Hart for the next 13 years, until his death.

This intrepid stereo photographer used this little vessel to travel on the Ocklawaha River, take photographs, and then, to develop them, he lowered the side curtains to create a darkroom.

This Palatka scene shows *Lollie Boy,* a local St. Johns vessel; *Forester,* an occasional Ocklawaha River vessel; and *Ocklawaha* at the right. Bricks are stacked in the right foreground.

Seven

THE HART LINE
DOMINATES

Osceola had the distinction of transporting General U.S. Grant on his 1880 trip upon the Ocklawaha River. No photos have been found of Grant aboard *Osceola*. Winter visitors pose in this view.

The visitors pictured here are either dressed for the cold winter weather or to impress their fellow passengers. Only middle- and upper-class persons could afford to take a winter vacation.

The crew of the *Osceola* poses for this picture; their cargo is on the bank at right. This photograph was taken in early 1886 by George Barker, an award-winning photographer from Buffalo, New York.

Eureka was a local service vessel at Silver Springs. With no sleeping accommodations on board, she was of limited use and surely was not a handsome vessel.

Osceola is pictured here at Silver Springs. *Eureka* (center) and *Wahoo* (right) are in the background. Both were local boats based at Silver Springs.

The strange device atop the *Osceola*'s pilot house is an iron pan with a rear reflector. Pine knots were placed in this and lit at night in order to illuminate the surrounding woods.

Tourists pose on the *Osceola*, which has been slightly rebuilt at this point in time. Ropes have been added to the railings for safety.

This view of the Silver Springs dock in the 1880s shows *Eureka* at left and *Okahumkee* at right.

An 1885 scene at Silver Springs includes *Eureka*, on the left, and *Wahoo*, on the right. These vessels were used on local day trips around the area.

This night view shows how pine knots were placed in baskets outside the vessel. Later on, the pine knots were placed in a iron pan atop the pilot house.

Ocklawaha steamboat captains often performed errands for the people living along the river. Here, an exchange is taking place. This 1871 illustration shows a very crude sidewheeler, but recessed sternwheelers were the norm.

HART'S DAILY LINE

OF

OCKLAWAHA RIVER STEAMERS.

Str. Okeehunkee, Str. Osceola,

CAPT. A. L. RICE, CAPT. D. A. DUNHAM,

Leave PALATKA at 9 A. M.

FOR SILVER SPRING, LEESBURG, AND OKEEHUNKEE.

H. L. HART, Proprietor and Agent.

Tickets on sale with LEVE & ALDEN, 271 Broadway, New York, and at their Agencies.

Misspelling and all (*Okeehunkee*), this is an advertisement for Hart's Daily Line in the 1880s. Captain David A. Dunham supervised construction and repairs to Hart Line vessels.

Osceola cautiously pokes her way through the dense foliage on the Ocklawaha River. This early 1886 photograph was taken by George Barker, who visited Florida in 1886 from the Buffalo, New York, Niagara Falls area.

Eight

SILVER SPRINGS

A boating party poses for a photograph at Silver Springs. All are dressed for cooler weather, wearing hats and warm clothing.

The long-lived *Okahumkee*, also spelled *Okeehumkee*, was a fixture on the river for several decades. She was added to over the years and is shown above in her earliest version. Note the stacked wood fuel in the photo below.

Groups of visitors pose on the *Okeehumkee*. These photos were taken at the beginning of a trip, developed, and then sold to passengers at the end of the trip.

The *Okahumkee* eventually had her pilot house moved to the top of the upper deck. Note the stairs, baggage, and horizontal rope restraints in this image.

Okahumkee is docked at a landing; notice the wood fuel on the left and the musical instrument on the right. Travelers would often "sing along" with the crew in the evening.

Okeehumkee is pictured here at Palatka, above, and at a river landing, below. Her pilot house is placed forward on her second cabin deck.

Okeehumkee passengers stretch their legs ashore at a landing while the crew takes on wood.

This stern view of *Okeehumkee* shows how the water discharged from the recessed stern paddlewheel exits the vessel at the stern.

A full load of posing passengers travel on the long-lived *Okeehumkee*.

Logs were often rafted on the Ocklawaha River. Here, *Okeehumkee* ties up near such a raft.

Okeehumkee is seen here at Silver Springs shortly after the turn of the century. The springs were the premier tourist attraction in Florida.

This is a classic head-on view of *Okeehumkee* at Silver Springs. The vessel's captain is at top right, and two crew members are in front, on the cargo deck.

An old stereo view shows *Okahumkee* on the picturesque Ocklawaha River.

Tuskawilla was one of the
"prettiest" steamboats
on the river. She had a
polygonal pilot house
and carved balustrades
as shown here. Some of
the visitors carry dummy
rifles, usually given out as
props for a photograph.

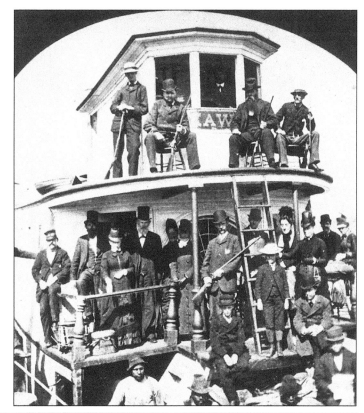

Tuskawilla was built by Jacksonville doctor/dentist, S.J. Bouknight, and is seen here at Agnew's
turpentine still along the river.

A beautiful side view of *Tuskawilla* is highlighted in this image. Note the skylights over the cabin.

Tuskawilla passengers pose for the mandatory photograph. *Tuskawilla* did not run on the river for many years.

Waunita did not run long on the river; she had twin stacks, an ornamental pilot house, an oval front window, and, all in all, a rather dainty appearance.

The *Astatula* was the only Hart vessel that had a fenced walkway around the pilot house and upper deck quarters, thus affording passengers room to stretch their legs.

An 1895 photo of *Astatula* features the vessel's two decks of passenger accommodations. Note the homemade flagstaff that served to helped guide these vessels on the twisty Ocklawaha.

Astatula is being tied up at a way landing on the river in order to take on wood fuel. She always appeared to be top-heavy.

It was a weird sight to see boats coming through the swamps with a wood fire on top to light the way, according to the press of the day. Note that the rear door is open to let water escape from the inboard recessed sternwheel.

Dr. Clarence B. Moore, a prominent archaeologist, owned the *Alligator*, which he used to store the Indian antiquities he excavated along many Southern rivers. *Alligator* was never on regular service on the Ocklawaha, however.

Nine

ED LUCAS'S METAMORA

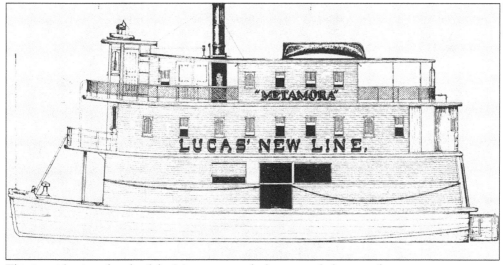

This is a side view sketch of the *Metamora*, made from actual photographs.

Ed Lucas of Palatka built the *Metamora* in 1893 to compete directly with the Hart Line, and this vessel did afford formidable opposition at times. On other occasions, Lucas and Hart combined their advertising to minimize competition.

This 1902 photo shows *Metamora* easing her way around a sinuous bend of the river. Note the closeness of the bordering trees and aquatic vegetation.

Metamora is pictured at Silver Springs in 1902. Note the barrels of naval stores that *Metamora* will load. A glass-bottomed, sightseeing boat is at left. She will take visitors who want to view the underwater sights in the clear waters of the springs.

Rounding a river bend, *Metamora* stops momentarily to have her picture taken by a Palatka photographer.

Metamora is pictured again at Silver Springs. Her white-garbed cook takes a break.

Metamora filled with water and, unexpectedly, sunk one night in 1903 while rounding a bend on the Ocklawaha River. Two young crew members were drowned. These were the only known fatalities on the river.

Metamora's recessed sternwheel throws out water as she proceeds on her Ocklawaha River journey.

The 1903 *Hiawatha* was the last steamboat built for the Hart Line. Hart died in December 1895, but his brother-in-law took over the business and successfully ran it for another two decades.

Hiawatha is seen here at Silver Springs after the turn of the century. Railroads had begun to take away some of the visitors who had previously used Ocklawaha River steamboats to reach Silver Springs.

Ten

LAST DAYS

This view of Silver Springs shows the competition between railroads and Ocklawaha River vessels such as *Hiawatha* (center) and *William Howard* (to the left).

A touched-up photo has birds placed judiciously to form additional interest for this *Hiawatha* postcard of the early 1900s.

A daytime photo of the *Hiawatha* has been touched up to create the illusion of a nighttime shot, with the illumination of the pine knots and the "ghostly" effect. These were popular Florida postcards of the early 20th century.

The last commercial steamboat to run on the river was *William Howard*, shown here with a good cargo of cotton and bagged goods.

William Howard is pictured here at Silver Springs in the 1920s. Railroads are on the other side of the combination depot and storage area. The steamboat era would soon come to its end.

This 1905 view of the *William Howard* shows a deckhand at the bow, spearing fish for a morning meal. Passengers often feasted on freshly caught fish.

William Howard was owned and built by the Howards of Grahamville, Florida. This stern view shows the open "rear door" of the vessel, where water was discharged.

William Howard was sold by the Howards and renamed *Tourist* by her new owners. She was also lengthened 20 feet and is shown in this simulated nighttime view, which was printed as a color postcard.

In 1919, the Hart Line ceased operations. Their *Okeehumkee* was tied up at the Hart's Point shipyard in East Palatka and was dismantled in the late 1930s. These photos were taken in the 1930s.

The Hart Line's *Hiawatha* was hauled out of the water in 1919 on the marine railway where she was built. Over the years, she slowly rotted away. This photo was taken in the 1940s.

This was truly the end of the line; *Hiawatha* is seen here in the 1960s (top) and the 1970s (bottom). The remains of the vessel were burned in 1978 and a condominium complex named "Hiawatha" was built on the property.